GW00383080

"A society without humor
is no laughing matter."

THE JAPANESE
A FIELD GUIDE

OBSERVATIONS BY
TIM ERNST AND MIKE MARKLEW

THE JAPANESE : A FIELD GUIDE
©1992 by Tim Ernst & Mike Marklew
All rights reserved.

Japanese Translation: Masako Marklew

First Edition: November 1992

Published by The Japan Times, Ltd.
5-4, Shibaura 4-chome, Minato-ku, Tokyo 108, Japan

Printed in Japan

To Masako with our heartfelt gratitude

Foreword

A few months ago, a pair of distinguished humo(u)rists were having a few beers together at the Tokyo British Club. They were Tim Ernst the American cartoonist/illustrator and Mike Marklew the British writer/columnist. Their conversation ranged over topics as far apart as molecular physics to geopolitics and finally arrived at the conclusion that what this country really needed was a good field guide to the native inhabitants.

"Well, being a couple of expats married to two lovely Japanese ladies and being the fathers of three little 'double kids,' we considered ourselves qualified Nihonjin observers. So, after toasting to our new-found recognition, we decided to collaborate on a project to rectify the lack of this guide. Thus, *'The Japanese: A Field Guide'* was born.

"Of course the birth of an idea is the easy part, actually producing it is somewhat more difficult. We needed a format and after a few more beers we discovered that we both had a common interest in 'bird watching'—even the feathered variety.

(Remember, after a few beers, anything sounds funny!) So, we decided to set the format in the style of a scientific field guide to the native ornithology. Here, on the pages to follow is the culmination of years of Nihonjin observation, laid out as 'a field guide to native birds.'

"We would like to thank the many thousands of Japanese who willingly or unknowingly allowed us to observe them in their natural habitat, doing what comes naturally. We also want to thank our wives for boldly stepping out, beyond the perimeters of the accepted norms and marrying two bird-brain gaijin like us. And finally, our thanks to our Editors and Publisher for their vision and gamble on us."

Tim Ernst & Mike Marklew

Disclaimer

This book is intended to be a humorous depiction of Japanese society at large, without any malice toward anybody. Except for the caricatures of the authors (Observers) and those of their children (WAA Children), any resemblance to persons living or dead of the characters depicted herein, is purely coincidental. All caricatures and characters in this book are fictitious, the product of the author(s)' imagination. No attempt was made to stereotype, degrade or belittle any profession, member of either sex, or peculiarities inherent in any society. References of an ornithological nature were made merely to add humor to the descriptions and to give the book the "sense" of a zoological field guide. We apologize in advance to anyone offended by our book. We apologize to any birds as well. It is our fervent hope that all will laugh and enjoy reading this book as much as we have laughed and enjoyed making it.

The authors

THE JAPANESE
A FIELD GUIDE

The Taxi Driver

Unusually polite and don't ask for tips. Often talk too much if you say anything in Japanese. Can read signs, but tend to get lost. Found everywhere in abundant supply but difficult to catch when raining or between midnight and 3 a.m. Nests are scrupulously clean. Have been known to unintentionally maim foreigners with their automatic doors!

【タクシーの運転手】すこぶる礼儀正しく、チップを要求する性質はない。もし日本語でちょっとでも話しかけられようものなら、えんえんとおしゃべりを続けるのも特徴。いたるところ無数に生息するが、雨の日と深夜〜午前3時に捕獲するのは困難である。彼らの巣はきわめて清潔に保たれている。しばしば自動ドアでガイジンを痛い目にあわせる事は、つとに有名。意図的ではないようだが……。

The Arubaito (Part Timer)

Spawned by the arrival of fast food chains (pre-Disneyland), they speak in a form of coded English and even the males have ultra-high pitched voices. Never appear to be older than their teens, this breed changes color from pale to darkly tanned for one month after the ski season and summer holiday season when they migrate to the Japanese Alps or Hawaii respectively. Always effervescent.

【アルバイター】ファーストフード・チェーンの日本上陸（前ディズニーランド時代）と共に繁殖した人種。暗号的英語をあやつり、男性でもカン高い声を張り上げる。決して10代以上の年齢には見えないこの種族、スキーシーズンと夏休みには日本アルプスやらハワイやらへ移動する習性あり。しかるに1か月後、小麦色の肌に変貌している。年間を通し、異常に活動的である。

The O.L.

Usually be-suited in daylight, but difficult to distinguish at night. Swarm at lunchtime. All have startlingly straight hair and never smoke in the office. Specialize in making tea or coffee, emptying ashtrays and garbage bins, handwriting envelopes, typing letters in *kanji,* answering the telephone and greeting arriving visitors. Rarely reach executive status—most often get married and quit.

【OL】 昼間はたいていスーツ姿なので見分けられるが、夜間になると識別しがたい。ランチタイムに一群となって出歩く習性がある。主な活動はお茶くみ・灰皿やゴミ箱のそうじ・封筒のあて名書き・文書の漢字タイプ・電話と来客の応対など。管理職につく者はまれで、多くは結婚退職していく。

The "Average" Salaryman

Easily seen in vast sleepy hordes in the morning. All wear dark suits with company lapel badge and white shirts. Beware of those who smell of garlic. Married ones often spend at least two hours every day travelling, rarely eat at home on weeknights and at weekends perform "famirii sābisu" by sleeping in late or taking the family out in their cars. Become prematurely grey on leaving university and all smoke cigarettes.

【平均的サラリーマン】朝方、寝ボケまなこで群れをなしているから、発見はたやすい。社章バッジを付けたねずみ色の背広にワイシャツのいでたち。ニンニク臭のキツイ者も多いので注意すべし。すでにづがいになっている者は最低2時間通勤に費やすため、平日は夜も外食が多い。週末には昼ごろまで寝ていたり家族とドライブという「家族サービス」なる行動を取る。大学を出るや否やねずみ色に変色し、皆タバコを吸う人種である。

The Businessman and "Daughter"

Found in exclusive coffee houses, expensive boutiques, even more expensive restaurants, hotel lobbies or spas and in the "Superior Seating" (Green Seat) cars of the bullet trains, they never touch each other in public and communication is usually in lowered voices. The males are most often corporate executives and their "daughters" are not.

【ビジネスマンと「娘」と称する女】お高そうな喫茶店やブティック、さらには超高級レストランやホテルのロビー・温泉・列車の「特別席（グリーン車）」などで見かけられる人々。人前ではよそよそしいくらいに振る舞い、たいていひそひそ声で話している。男は会社の重役などが多く、「娘」と称する方はそうではないようだ。

18

The Early Morning Aspiring Baseball Star

Can be found by dawn's light on any vacant tract of land or rooftop, performing a Japanese club swinging ritual, which has become the native version of jogging. Some anthropologists claim this baseball ritual is instilled at birth by their fathers watching too many TV ballgames, however others believe it comes from a strong desire to "strike out" at society in general or their boss and mother-in-law in particular.

【早朝練習に励むプロ志望の野球選手】明け方から野球の素振りに没頭する集団をよく見るが、これはジョギングの日本版ともいえるもの。この野球熱は父親がテレビの野球中継を見すぎていたことによる先天性のもの、と唱える人類学者もいる。だが別の学説によれば、世の中、特に上司や義母への反抗心の表れという。

The Bonsaist

Specialize in producing trees, plants and shrubs in a dwarflike scale. This species is an absolute necessity in a land where city houses are often tiny and rarely have any garden. Because most natives sleep on the floor, it is still possible to look up through the branches of a bonsaied pine tree. Bonsaied orange trees produce astonishingly acerbic fruit but the flowers are cute!

【ボンサイスト】あらゆる木を小人サイズに作り変える専門家。人々の住む家があまりに小さく庭もろくにないこの地では、不可欠な存在とされる。なぜならタタミにふとんで寝ていれば、盆栽の松の木であっても見上げることができるからだ。みかんの木を盆栽にすると実はまずくて食べられる代物ではないが、花はたいへんカワイイ。

Cackling Schoolgirls

Travel in packs and most wear sailor suits every day of the week. Although shorter than the male 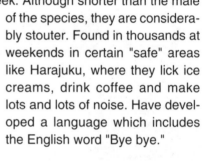 of the species, they are considerably stouter. Found in thousands at weekends in certain "safe" areas like Harajuku, where they lick ice creams, drink coffee and make lots and lots of noise. Have developed a language which includes the English word "Bye bye."

【キャピキャピやかましい女学生】平日はセーラー服に身を包み、集団で歩き回っている。この人種の男たちよりも背は低いが、横幅の方は負けず劣らず。一方休日になると原宿のような「安全」地域に群がり、アイスクリームをなめながらさらにけたたましい騒音を発する。この種族が作った言語には「バイビー」等あり。

The AV Girl

Part of their bodies appear to be of hazy construction, which can be observed when they divest themselves of their plumage—which they do quite often. Most only make throaty noises or emit squeaks. The ones which have learned the power of speech, often appear on late night TV, revealing their charms to a collection of men, one of whom is always wearing a peaked cap!

21

【AVギャル】頻繁に衣服を脱ぐのでよく観察できることだが、この人種の体は一部、かすんでボヤケている。たいていはあえぎ声や叫び声くらいで、言語らしきものは発達していない。人前で話す力を得ると深夜テレビに出演し、男たちに──いつも野球帽をかぶった映画カントクもその一人──媚を売るようになる。

The Kabuki Actor

Capable of instilling the most indescribable level of boredom in all except the most serious aficionado, these actors are all male and speak a strange language, painfully slowly. In kabuki theaters, an earphone translation service is available in English and in Japanese! A few have been made "Living National Treasures"—until they die. Being all male, it is believed they are created—not born.

【歌舞伎役者】熱狂的ファン以外にとっては耐えがたい退屈を与えてくれる役者たちで、全員が男性である。奇妙な声でおそろしくゆっくり話すのも特徴。歌舞伎劇場では英語ばかりか、日本語のイヤホン翻訳サービスまでやっている！　人間国宝になるものも多い。全員が男性ということは、この人種は生まれてくるのではなく、どこかで製造されているらしい。

Miss . . . (Idol)

Excruciatingly thin, incredibly young looking and often equipped with the worst set of teeth you've ever seen, most have virtually no talent. Their voices are so high pitched, dogs wince when they speak. Because this species is spawned by the publicity machine, they need no singing ability and they appear and disappear almost overnight.

【アイドル】やせぎすで幼なく、歯並びがひどいのも多い。おしなべて才能はないに等しいが、その金切り声は犬をもたじろがせるのであなどれない。マス・メディアによって大量生産されている彼女たちに歌唱力など必要なく、一夜にして現れては消える生き物である。

The Yakuza

Even though they all look the same, this breed is very clannish and often squabble among themselves over territorial matters. Their skins are often gaudily painted, both their hair and at least one little finger are cropped short, they wear dark glasses, gold chains, abuse the language and are very dangerous to approach, especially with phrases like, "Got a light mate!"

【ザ・ヤクザ】この人種は一見みな同じように見えるが、実は派閥どうしの抗争が激しく、シマをめぐってのいさかいなど日常茶飯事。趣味のよろしい彫り物を肌にほどこし、髪の毛と指の1〜2本は短かめが主流。サングラスと金のアクセサリーが好みで言葉づかいの荒っぽいこの人々に接近するのは、やや危険を伴なう行為である——特に、「火ィ借してくれませんか？」なんて言いながら近づくのは。

The Ginza Hostess

Nocturnal, they appear in the hundreds at 7:30 p.m. on week nights at Shinbashi, Ginza and Yurakucho stations and rush off to minute burrows to pour water into their customers' glasses. Always well coiffured and exquisitely dressed in designer clothes or kimono, they are rarely available for "hanky panky" being either married, having boyfriends or both. Disappear as suddenly as they appear at 11:30 p.m.

【銀座のホステス】夜行性動物。平日の夕方7時半ごろ新橋・銀座・有楽町の各駅にぞくぞくと現れ、それぞれの小さな巣穴へとかけ込む。客のグラスに水割りを作るためである。髪をきれいにセットし、高価なブランド服か着物に身を包む彼女たちは、めったに「オアソビ」の相手にはなってくれない。みんな夫か恋人、ときにはその両方がいるからだ。深夜11時半になると、来た時と同じくらい突然に姿を消す。

The Pachinko Manager

Easily distinguished by his carrying more keys than a Fort Knox jailer. His nest has more active neon light than the Ginza, Times Square and Picadilly Circus rolled into one. Rarely seen outside his natural habitat in daylight, but can be found in small night clubs after 11 p.m., usually in the company of members of the pruned pinky set and kimono clad hostesses. Never speaks.

【パチンコ店の店長】フォート・ノックス刑務所の看守よりもたくさんのカギ束を腰からぶら下げているゆえ、すぐそれとわかる。また、銀座とタイムズ・スクエアとピカデリー・サーカスが一緒になってかかっても負けそうなほど、彼の巣のネオンはギンギラギンである。昼間はめったに生息地以外へ出歩かないが、夜11時過ぎには小さなバーなどで見かけられ、小指がないお友達や着物のホステスに囲まれている。無口である。

The Simple Walkman

Magnetic tape operated native, often with noise emanating from its skull. Young ones produce sounds of tribal music however they often change to Mozart as they age. They maintain glazed eyes, but appear to be tuned to station name announcements when travelling on trains. Occasionally found as couples in parks—plugged together.

【(おつむが)超軽量ウォークマン】磁気テープであやつられている原住民。頭から騒音がもれていることが多い。若いうちは原始的部族音楽を好み、年をとるにつれモーツァルトを好む傾向がある。どんよりした目をしていながらも、電車では駅名のアナウンスを聞きのがさないよう注意している。公園ではカップルになったのも見かけられる――プラグで一つにつながって。

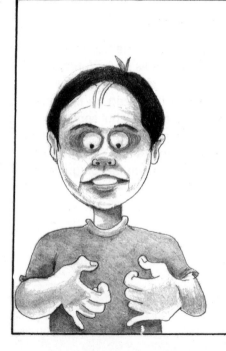

A Fami-con-aholic

These can be easily discovered because their eyes never stay still and their fingers always fidget. Younger members of this breed can be observed in almost any form of public transport, oblivious to the crowds. It is believed that the older ones who can be found in any "Game Parlor" were once station clippies who have been retired due to the introduction of automatic ticket wickets.

【ファミコン中毒者】目はキョロキョロ、指は絶えずせわしなく動いているので、とても見分けやすい。この種の若者はバスや電車で頻繁に見かけられる。一方「ゲーセン」に入りびたるややふけたのは、自動改札機導入により失職した、もと駅の改札係たちである、と言われている。

Friendly Deliveryman (enters automatically)

Probably created by the biannual, present-giving ritual, this breed will walk into any place unlocked in its efforts to divest itself of its package. Capable of cramming more items into tiny vehicles than the Guinness Book of Records can list. Clans have been formed with some allegedly nefarious government connections.

29

【親切すぎる宅配員】年に2度の贈答シーズンのため繁殖した彼らは、荷物から解放されたい一心でカギのかかっていない所にはどこでも入ってくる。小さなバンには、ギネスブックにも載せきれないほどの配達物を積み込んでいる。ある者は政府との癒着によって一大派閥を成したとか……。

The "Naitā" (Night Baseball) Fan

Dressed in the plumage of his favourite team, this species becomes glued to the television set while armed with two packs of cigarettes, a case of beer and assorted packs of shredded dried fish, or other strange snacks. Spawned by the fact, baseball game tickets sell out within minutes of being put on sale. Similar to other nation's "Couch Potatoes."

【ナイター・ファン】ひいきのチームの帽子やシャツを身につけ、ナイター中継があるとテレビに貼り付いてしまう。タバコとビール、さきいかなどの珍味が観戦に必須のアイテム。野球場の入場券が手に入りにくいことからはびこった人種とも言われる。どこかの国の「カウチポテト族」に類似点あり。

The Late Night Commuter

This breed can strap-hang and sleep at the same time. Both male and female, the species vary from office workers to students. Seated, if in a pair, they will sleep on each other's shoulders; if alone they will sleep on other's shoulders. They appear to have an inbred sixth sense which switches their eyes on precisely as they reach their home station. Often forget umbrellas, briefcases and sometimes their shoes.

【深夜通勤族】この生物には、つり革にぶら下がって眠れる特性がある。男も女もいれば、会社員から学生までと層も厚い。座っている場合、二人連れであれば互いの肩にもたれ合って眠る。だが連れがいなくとも、他人の肩を無断借用して、やはり眠るのである。彼らには第六感が備わっているらしく、自分の降りる駅でぱっと目を覚ます。忘れ物も得意で、カサや書類かばん、中にはクツまで忘れる者がいる。

The Fishmonger

Never seem to have any hair but nearly all need a shave. They are always loudly calling their wares, even if nobody is around. This has led to a mistaken belief that they talk to the fish. Can be discovered in their multitudes at Tsukiji market at 3 a.m. squabbling over the price of tuna.

【魚屋のオヤジ】 つるつる頭にうっすら無精ヒゲ、という手合いがなぜか多い。誰も通りかからなくても大声で呼び込みを続ける奇癖があるため、魚に話しかけているのではないか、と誤解されがち。毎日午前3時に築地へ群れ集まり、マグロの値段をせり合っている。

The Disneylander

Ageless, these are participants in a daily ritual gathering, where hundreds of thousands of them will arrive at exactly the same time, queue all day for a few minutes of excitement and then all depart for the far corners of the land—together. All wear some form of tribal costume varying from Mickey Mouse ears to caps with Donald Duck beaks, many with their names—in English, embroidered on them.

【ディズニーランダー】老いを知らない。毎日、儀式のごとく何万人となって開園時間きっかりに集まり、数分間の興奮のために一日中でも行列をつくるのである。しかるのち、広大な敷地のはるか彼方に見える次のアトラクションへと移動する——群れをなして。彼らの部族衣装は、ミッキーマウスのお耳やドナルドのくちばし付き帽子など多様。もちろん「お名前刺しゅうサービス」付きの代物である。

The Elevator Operator

Always in impeccable uniform, perfectly manicured with neat hairstyles, they spend their lives, pushing buttons, looking at the ground, bowing people in and out of the doors and reciting excitedly about the goodies on every floor. They use such a level of polite Japanese, many foreigners can understand them, even though most don't know one single word of English.

【エレベーターガール】非の打ちどころのない制服を着用し、マニキュアもヘアスタイルもバッチリ。ボタンを押し、床を見つめ、乗降客におじぎをし、各階の売り場案内を復唱するだけの日々である。彼女たちはたいへんきれいな日本語を使うため、外国人でも聞きとりやすいほど。しかし英語の方は……。

The Telephone Booth Stickers

Found in their hundreds in all entertainment districts, these are eagerly sought after by hawks of all ages. Often offering wildly exciting themes, they can also be quite disappointing. Some have featured the same chick on it for the last fifteen years! If you plan to collect some, please stick them back-to-back because the glue will not come off anything it adheres to!

【電話ボックスの広告シール】歓楽街のあらゆる電話ボックスに無数にばらまかれ、年齢に関係なく男性諸氏の視線をくぎづけにする。コピーは扇情的だが、実体はひどく期待はずれなのがほとんど。中には、写真の女性が15年間変わらないのもある！ これを収集したい向きにひとこと。このシールの接着力は非常に強力なので、2枚一組にして貼り合わせておくとグッド。

The Door-to-door Condom Saleswoman

Incredibly tenacious, they have always been a part of the scenery, however since the advent of AIDS they have additional things to say. Apparently become speechless if the person opening the door happens to be a foreigner—particularly if a partially clothed male. This breed may be dying out due to the increase in vending machines for their products.

【コンドームの訪問販売員】どんな時にも生き残ってきた、しぶといおばさんたち。昨今はエイズのため、セールストークもいっそう説得力を増した。しかし、玄関に出迎えたのがガイジン、それも半裸だったりすると、なぜか沈黙してしまう。自動販売機が普及したので、この種は絶滅の途をたどっているのかもしれない。

The PTA President

Always female, whose breeding (i.e. her husband's job) carries her above the status of the lesser parents. Have been known to create fear in school principals and make parents do amazing things like produce rice balls or lunch boxes for 500. Often have at least three gold teeth, usually wear fabulously expensive jewelry, tailored suits and never smoke.

【PTA会長】決まって女性である。その育ちのよさ(すなわち夫の職業のこと)によって、他の父母たちより上の地位についた。校長たちにとって脅威の存在であるばかりか、父母たちにも信じがたいことをやらせてしまう——例えば500人分のおにぎりや弁当を作るとか。金歯は3本くらいあるのがふつうで、身に着けるのは高そうな宝石類とオーダーメイドのスーツ。もちろん大の嫌煙家である。

The Civil Servant

Found in all government buildings and city authority offices. Basically of two types, helpful or decidedly unhelpful. All are masters of defensive speech, but often difficult to make speak at all. Usually seen wearing black plastic sleeve covers with two or more rubber tipped fingers. Will prey on the uninformed and those who have filled out the wrong forms.

【お役所の公務員】官庁や市・区役所に生息する。この人種は基本的に、2つに大別できる――親切なのと、底意地悪いくらい不親切なのとに。弁解にはたけているが、その他に関してはおしなべて口下手。両腕の黒い腕貫とゴムの指サックがトレードマーク。手続きのしかたがよくわからない人々と申請書に記入ミスをした人を徹底的に苦しめることで有名。

The New Generation

A new breed who have dropped the dull garb of the rest of the species and don't even wear ties. Often both sexes look identical, and they have even developed a new form of communication pattern to prevent the older generation from understanding what they are doing. The only time they are intelligible is when they are complaining about something, which they do most of the time.

【新人類】他の日本人のような無個性な服装はせず、むろんネクタイを嫌う。男も女も同じように見えるこの人種は、独自のコミュニケーション手段を使うので、旧人類には全く理解できない。しょっちゅう文句をこぼし、そんな時だけは他人に意志を伝えられるのだから理不尽。

The Traditional Squat

Performed from birth, this method of sitting is practiced by the whole species, irrespective of size, sex or age. Aged women can retain this position all day. Foreigners cannot execute this pose for more than a few minutes without experiencing excruciating pain in their legs for days afterward. The Japanese however, have mastered the art of keeping a straight face. Clinically observed, they may be suffering. Research continues!

【正座】体格や性別、年齢にかかわらず、この国の人々は生まれた時からこの座り方を練習している。年輩女性ともなると、朝から晩までこのまま座っていられる。もしガイジンが3分以上正座をしたならば、その後何日かは拷問のような痛みが足に残るだろう。しかし、日本人は感情を顔に表さないことでも有名である。臨床的見地から考えると、彼らもやはり苦痛を感じているのかもしれない。研究課題である。

The Punk

Once believed non-existent in Japan, this species has recently surfaced in areas like Tokyo's Yoyogi Park on Sundays. They appear to be attracted by the music in the park and also appear to be quite deaf. Although they look similar to punks of other lands, this species often talks in high-pitched voices and is usually docile—still, best avoided.

【パンク】以前は日本に存在しないと言われていたが、最近になって日曜の代々木公園あたりに出没する人種である。同公園の音楽に誘われて出てくるようだが、実は耳が遠いようでもある。外国のパンク野郎と見かけは変わらないものの、こちらは声にハクがなく、態度も従順。とはいえ、やたら近寄らないのが賢明だ。

The Tour Guide

Brightly colored plumage with hat and flag, there is one in front of every crowd and at the door of every tour bus. They can apparently see through the back of their heads and have learned how to talk continuously even if nobody is listening and when armed with electronic amplification can rouse the dead at any serene temple or shrine. Always smell of soap.

【観光ガイド】目の覚めるような色の制服で手には旗を持ち、観光客をゾロゾロひき連れていたり、観光バスの入口で待ち受けている。自分の背後の風景を透視できるだけでなく、誰も聞いていなくてもしゃべり続ける能力がある。アンプの力を借りれば、静まりかえった寺に眠る死者をも起こすという。いつも石鹸の匂いがする。

The Kabukicho Hostess

Similar to the Ginza breed, also nocturnal, but talk more and drink real liquor. Plumage is either gaudy or very simple, but always easy to remove. Often can cater to other needs of their customers, are sometimes seen prowling in the early hours and many can speak English. Beware, most have short-fingered patrons.

【歌舞伎町のホステス】銀座のホステスと同じく夜行性ながら、はるかによくしゃべり、よく飲む。衣装は派手なのも地味なのもいるが、いずれにせよカンタンに脱いでしまうという。客のニーズで出前もするのか、まだ早い時間に徘徊していることも。英語を話す者も少なくない。注意すべきは、指の短かいパトロン付きが多い点。

The Ticket Puncher

Restless, nervous, forever clicking to some unheard melody in its head with a rhythm akin to some ancient cult dance, this species is dying out. Punch drunk to the point of never looking at faces, it can spot an underpaid fare in a flash. As automatic ticket wickets take over in the cities, they are all migrating to the countryside.

【駅の改札係】原始的な宗教舞踊に似た音楽をその脳裏で奏でながら、休みなく神経質にハサミを鳴らす人種。ハサミの使いすぎによるパンチドランカーで、人の顔すらろくに見ていない。なのにキセルは瞬時に見分けられるのだから、タダモノではない。自動改札機が普及する昨今、地方へと大移動しているようである。

44

The Dinosaur

Never grow taller than 5 feet and appear to hate foreigners, it is believed that this species hates everyone because there is never any smile to be seen. Because they smell of moth balls, anthropologists conclude that they are in fact ancient samurai, who have committed some awful crime against the Gods and have been left on Earth to atone.

【化石人間】 身長は150センチ以下。大のガイジン嫌いだが、この人種はしょせん誰もかれも嫌いらしい。どんな時もニコリともしないのがその証拠。ショウノウ臭いことから、実は彼らは昔々何か大罪を犯したサムライで、罪ほろぼしのためにあの世へ成仏できないのだ、と学者たちは言っている。

The Stud

Although similar in build to foreign species, these are not your usual hulk. During daylight may be observed in parks doing ritual exercises, but at night are mostly to be discovered in Host Bars with middle aged, rich, female patrons. Not at all threatening and to most visitors of both sex, they look "cute"!

【セクシーボーイ】肉体的には外国の同類と共通点はあるが、こちらの方はムキムキゴリラではない。日中は公園などでシェイプアップに励み、夜になるとホストクラブで金満オバさまの相手になったりする。危険性はなく、男性客からも女性客からも「カワイーイ!」と言われてしまう。

Ojō-san

Cool, this breed is either alone or found in identical groups who all maintain a very high opinion of themselves. Doll-like in their own minds, if spoken to, will force a smile, but usually will not make any reply. Always turn out to be somebody's aunt, never marry, or are already divorced. It is unknown if they actually work.

【中年お嬢様】つねに冷静で孤高を保ち、たまに付き合う友達といったら鼻もちならないテングばかり。ふだんは人形のようにすかしている。話しかけられれば作り笑いを浮かべるが、ろくに答えもしない。一生独身主義、でなければすでに出戻りというのが多い。いったい何か仕事をしているのかどうか、よくわからない人種である。

48

The Stockbroker

Boom or bust this breed never changes expression. They appear to work all day and night, however a few can be spotted in early morning trains going home or around midnight in all-night noodle stalls. Nowhere near as wealthy as their foreign counterparts, they do however exude the air of comfortableness and are all married.

【証券マン】景気の良し悪しにかかわらず、表情を変えない人々。24時間働いているようだが、ときどき早朝の始発電車や深夜のラーメン屋で見かけられる。他の国の同業者のようなリッチぶりにはとても及ばないが、暮らし向きは悪くなく、ほとんどが既婚者である。

The Igo Master

This master of a game with 19^{19} possible permutations, is capable of sitting almost motionless for hours, without food and without saying anything. The click of the stones on the thick wooden board is music to his ears. It is believed masters can recall any one of 123,456,789 international, direct dial telephone numbers—instantly.

【碁の名人】 19の19乗通りもの順列をあやつるゲームの達人たる者、何時間ものあいだ食事もせずものも言わず、微動だにせず座っていられるのである。碁盤に打たれる石の音が、彼の耳には音楽となる。国際直通電話の9ケタの番号など、即座に暗記できてしまうのだ。

The Ultra Left/Right

Mostly male hawks, this breed travels about in re-conditioned riot police buses, equipped with loudspeakers whose level is set a few decibels above the threshold of pain. Unintelligible—even to the natives. Usually in hiding, but become very active whenever there are visiting VIPs from overseas. Will form long, noisy but very orderly rallies, where they are usually surrounded by a police force outnumbering them ten to one.

【極左／極右】改造された装甲車に乗り、拡声器でがまんできない騒音を流す男たちのこと。同じ日本人でさえ、彼らが何を言っているのかよくわからないと言う。ふだんはどこかにひそんでいるが、外国のＶＩＰが来日するたびに、やたらと活動的になる。自分たちよりはるかに多い警官たちに囲まれると従順になるが、やかましさは変わらない。

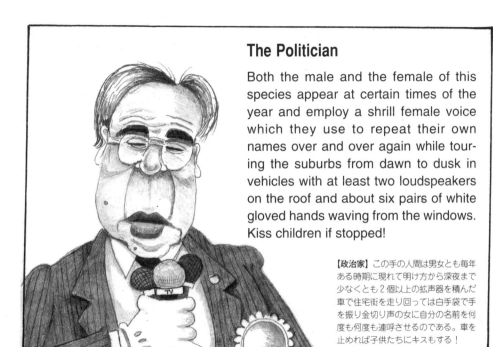

The Politician

Both the male and the female of this species appear at certain times of the year and employ a shrill female voice which they use to repeat their own names over and over again while touring the suburbs from dawn to dusk in vehicles with at least two loudspeakers on the roof and about six pairs of white gloved hands waving from the windows. Kiss children if stopped!

【政治家】この手の人間は男女とも毎年ある時期に現れて明け方から深夜まで少なくとも2個以上の拡声器を積んだ車で住宅街を走り回っては白手袋で手を振り金切り声の女に自分の名前を何度も何度も連呼させるのである。車を止めれば子供たちにキスもする！

The Lesser Obnoxious Drunk

Found in ones and twos on most late night transport, this breed has developed the ability to go to sleep at an angle, and then fall sideways onto the seat. Most are equipped with the same sixth sense as the late night commuter in being able to sense their home station. Those who don't, are eased off the train at the terminus by the vigilant station staff.

【あまり害のない酔っぱらい】深夜の電車には必ず1人か2人いる。ある傾斜角度で眠りに落ち、そのまま座席にズルズルと倒れこむという芸当ができる。深夜通勤族と同様、自分の降りる駅で起きられる第六感を備えている。そうでない者は、終点で親切な駅員さんによって運び出されることになる。

The Greater Obnoxious Drunk

This breed should be avoided at all costs. Surrounded by a pungent aroma, they are quick to take umbrage at nothing, often throw up and are normally very noisy. Usually alone, they will make a beeline for young girls on a train or try their best to teach any handy foreigner the Japanese language, by shouting at him or her. Advice: Change carriages.

【たいへん害のある酔っぱらい】この連中とは決して
かかわり合わない事。強烈なニオイをまき散らし、何
でもないことに腹を立て、吐くわわめくわで手に負え
ない。連れのいない場合が多いので、若い女の子にし
つこくからむか、でなければ都合よく居合わせたガイ
ジンに日本語のレッスンを始める。どちらにせよ大変
やっかいである。アドバイス：車輌をかえること。

54

The Ruby-throated Karaoke Singer

The songbirds of the species, of both sexes, these can be heard long before they are seen. They are electronicly amplified, but unable to carry a tune and the sound becomes louder and more intolerable when "singing" as a duet or trio. Gather together in small flocks who are oblivious to the noise. Unfortunately, not under immediate threat of extinction and can sometimes be seen on beaches, in parks and even foreign countries.

【カラオケ・ファン】男女を問わずこのカラオケ鳥たちは、はるか彼方にいてもやかましくてそれとわかってしまう。アンプの力を借りても、調子っぱずれは治るものではない。デュエットやトリオになると、そのうるささはガマンの限界を越える。騒音に鈍感な者どうしで仲間を作っている。残念ながら彼らは当分絶滅しそうにないどころか、海辺や公園、果ては海外へも生息分布を広げてしまった。

Female Wrestlers

Varying in size from elephantine to the GoodYear blimp, some are fairly attractive while others are absolutely, horrendously ugly. The former are usually nasty, while the latter are often quite sweet. After giving up the wrestling ring will quite often become "talent" singers—meaning they can't sing or act.

【女子プロレスラー】象みたいなのからアリんこまでサイズはさまざまで、容姿もカワイイのもいればシャレにならないほどひどいのもおり、極端である。可愛い方が意地悪で、ブスの方がけなげだったりする。引退後は「タレント」となる場合が多いが、それはつまり歌も演技もできないという意味である。

The Honeymooners

Swarm in pairs at airports migrating to the ritual breeding grounds of Hawaii, San Francisco, Sydney, Guam and Saipan. Always return in identical plumage without suntans, but with thousands of photographs so they can remember why they cannot afford to buy a nest, as well as at least two hundred packs of presents, one for every single person whom they know.

【ハネムーナー】ハワイやサンフランシスコ、シドニー、グアム、サイパンへと、子作りの儀式に旅立つべく空港にあふれかえる新婚カップルたちのこと。一目でそれとわかる服装で、日焼けも控えめに帰国する――親戚や知人に配る200個以上のお土産と、何枚もの写真をたずさえて。そしてその写真は後日、なぜ新居を買えなかったかの理由の一つとして役立つのである。

Sumō-tori

A classic of the species, considered by all in the flock to be some form of deity, they perform a ritual dance, which has had more written about it than any other dance on earth. Eat the most amazing amount of seed. When marry, tend to attract tiny females and produce normal-sized offspring. It is unknown how they mate.

【相撲とり】この国の在来種であり、どこか神格化されている存在。この宗教儀式めいた舞踊について、他のどんなダンスをもしのぐ数の出版物が出ている。信じられないほどよく食べる。なぜか結婚相手はとても小柄な女性が多く、その結果生まれてくるのは平均サイズの子供たち。しかしいったいどうやって作ったのか、知る由もない。

Late Night Video Rental Clerk

Although often exceedingly ferocious looking, they are invariably mild and very pale colored. Adroit at putting the wrong video into a carrying box, they are usually quite incapable of actually pronouncing the English titles on the tapes, relying on the *katakana* version. This makes it almost impossible to order any film which contains an L or a V in the title.

【真夜中のレンタルビデオ店の店員】オソロシげな風貌の者が多いが、実は柔和な人柄で、肌もひよわに青白い。まちがって別のテープを貸し出しケースに入れてしまうのはお手のものだが、洋画の原題はよく読めないのでカタカナに頼りがち。おかげでLやVの入っている題名の洋画ビデオを彼らに探してもらうのは、至難のワザなのである。

58

Late Night Video Renter

Furtive, this species can often be seen, scurrying home with their spoils clutched tightly to their chests, eyes downcast. Usually lone shoppers, they skulk about the concealed part of the video store, never look at the clerk and pay for their merchandise without checking the contents of the pack.

【真夜中のレンタルビデオ店の客】やっとの思いで借り出したビデオをしっかと胸に抱き、コソコソと伏し目がちに、しかし物凄いスピードで家路を急ぐ。たいがい一人で店にやってきて、秘密めいた奥の一角に隠れるように入っていく。ぜったい店員と視線を合わせず、ケースの中身も確認しないで料金を払って出ていってしまう。

The Company Volleyball Star

Absolutely incapable of doing any office work other than answering the telephone, this breed is reserved for corporate image enhancement. Far too tall to sit with its legs under the average Japanese table, they develop a permanent stoop if left off the volleyball pitch for too long. Seem to disappear around the age of 30.

【女子社会人バレーボールのエース】電話をとること以外の事務は全くできないものの、企業イメージ向上のために有用とされている。足が長すぎて日本の事務机には座ることができず、またバレーの試合をしばらく休むと、猫背が直らなくなってしまう。30歳前後で姿を消していく人たち。

The Neighborhood Gossip Monger

Appear to be equipped with the most acute sense of hearing, this breed can hear a rumor drop at 80 meters (50 yards) and can pass a message around a district in 10 seconds. Prior to the advent of newspapers, they were the only form of mass communication in Japan. Always married to diminutive husbands who do the housework, some of whom can actually knit.

【近所の「人間フライデー」】異常に発達した聴覚があり、80メートル向こうでこぼれ落ちたウワサ話を、10秒後には近所中に言いふらしてしまう。新聞がなかった時代には、日本唯一のマスコミ機関であった。彼女たちの亭主は風采のあがらないタイプで、家事ばかりか編み物までやってしまう男も少なくない。

The Housewife

Often quite invisible to visiting foreigners, this hen rules the roost in most nests, often controlling the purse, always controlling the education and feeding of the chicks and quite oblivious to the late arrival home of the roster although she sometimes hen-pecks. Often wear an apron and rarely are seen far from the nest except at neighborhood shops or local festivals.

【主婦】短期滞在のガイジンには視野に入らない存在。しかしこのメンドリたちの権力は絶大で、巣の中をとりしきり、ヒヨコらの教育やエサはもちろん、財布まで管理している場合が多い。オンドリを尻に敷いている割りには、彼らの帰宅が遅いのにはあまり文句を言わない。エプロン姿の彼女たちは、近所の買い物と地元のお祭り以外、めったに巣から離れようとしない。

The Sushiya

Never speak. They are dressed in hospital white and bear hands as scrupulously clean as any surgeon. Can wield a scalpel of monstrous size and slice through raw fish so thinly the result is transparent. Construct works of art with bits of assorted seafood atop hand shaped vinegared rice blocks. This breed is highly sought after among foreign health food fanatics.

【寿司職人】決して口をきかない。白衣をまとい、外科医にも劣らぬ清潔な手をしている。巨大なメスを振りかざし、透けるほどの薄さに魚を切ってみせる。寿司めしを四角ににぎってさまざまな魚の小片をのせ、彼らの芸術は完成する。海外のヘルシー・フード偏執狂たちの崇拝の対象でもある。

The Receptionist

The first and last thing you see when entering or leaving any place in Japan. Usually wearing some type of corporate plumage, this species specializes in sitting bold upright and pointing the way. They bear beautifully manicured claws, far too long to allow them to type and operate push button telephones with pencil ends.

【受付嬢】日本中どんな所に行っても、最初と最後に必ず出くわす女性たちのこと。企業の制服に身を包む彼女たちは、背すじを伸ばして座り続けることと方向を指さすことの専門職である。美しくマニキュアをほどこしたそのツメがあまりに長いので、タイプはもちろん打てないし、プッシュホンすら鉛筆の頭を使わざるをえない。

The Spoilt Brat

Some people believe this species of chick came about due to the influence of foreign television, however research has proved they have always been in existence. Most often, turn out to be the offspring of the only person in Japan whom you have to respect and be nice to. Their clothing is always designer brand and worn so that the label is visible.

【かわいげのないガキ】欧米のテレビ番組などの悪影響でこういうガキどもが増えたと言う人もいるが、このタイプは昔からいたのである。金持ちの実力者が父親である場合が多い。当然ブランドものしか着ず、それもブランド名がよく見えるように着るところが、実にカワイクない。

The Rock Star

Outrageous, multicolored plumage and clothing which is either four sizes too large or exceedingly tight. Imitate other nations' songbirds—sometimes better than the original sounds. Gather in their multitudes in places like the east edge of Yoyogi Park on Sundays where they try to out-db each other to the great delight of hordes of school kids.

【ロッカー】 ブカブカか、でなければピッタリ体にはりつくような、悪趣味で極彩色の服を好む。外国のミュージシャンの真似が多く、中には本人たちよりうまいのもいる。日曜の代々木公園にたくさん現れ、耳をつんざく大音響で演奏して少年少女を狂喜させている。

66

The Doctor

High on the pecking order of society, this breed does not answer questions—even, "What time is it?" Will dispense more pills, potions and powder than you can carry in one bag with the words, "X will fix the ailment, Y will fix side effects of X, Z will fix side effects of Y and A is just to make you feel good." Live in well padded nests.

【医者】社会的地位があまりに高いせいか、平民の質問にはぜったい答えない——たとえそれが「今、何時ですか?」であっても。患者のバッグに入りきらないほどたくさんのクスリを処方して、こう言うのだ。「X剤は病気を治して、Y薬はX剤の副作用防止。Y薬の副作用はZ錠でおさえます。さらにA薬を飲めば、だいぶ気分がよくなりますよ」。豪華な巣に住んでいる。

Monday Morning Zombies

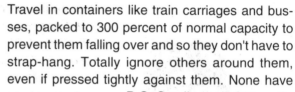

Travel in containers like train carriages and busses, packed to 300 percent of normal capacity to prevent them falling over and so they don't have to strap-hang. Totally ignore others around them, even if pressed tightly against them. None have B.O. Smells per 1,000: nothing 200, tobacco 800, soap and/or shampoo 500, garlic or stale booze 20, perfume 0.00001.

【月曜の朝のゾンビ】乗車率300%の超満員電車に乗っているおかげで、よろける心配もつり革につかまる必要もない人々。デオドラント・スプレーのさわやかな香りがする人ゼロ。1,000人中；無臭200人、タバコ臭いの800人、シャンプーの匂い500人、ニンニクか昨夜の酒臭いの20人、香水0.00001人（重複回答あり）。

The Living Treasure

A very highly respected member of the species who are quite old and always wear kimono which appear to be of similar age. Unkempt or bald, they all smoke, rarely smile and often talk in very ancient tongues so that on TV interviews it is necessary to have subtitles. They are endangered because they appear to die out faster than they are created.

【人間国宝】国民にとっても尊敬されている高齢の人たちで、みんなキモノを着ている。クシャクシャ髪かハゲ頭、そして一様に愛煙家。彼らは昔の言葉をつかうので、テレビのインタビューでは字幕が必要となる。毎年新しく人間国宝になる人数よりも多く他界してしまうため、少数生物である。

The Pocket Phone Jack

This breed is on the increase and can be often found standing totally still in the middle of the sidewalk, chattering incessantly. Other times they are usually caught standing by windows, even in expensive nightclubs and respond to bleeps like Pavlov's dog. They have been recently banned from using their skills in most posh restaurants.

【携帯電話男】急増中のこの人種、人混みの真っ只中に立ちはだかり、えんえんとしゃべり続けるツワモノである。屋内においては、たとえ高級クラブにいても窓際に立ち通しで、発信音にパブロフの犬のごとく反応する。スノッブなレストランでは、大変ひんしゅくをかっている人々。

The Education Mama

Filled with competitive instinct, this breed tends to smother their chicks with learning. Unsatisfied with a simple school curriculum, will force their chicks to attend pre-school school, after-school school and night school. Offspring can often be found asleep standing up on late night and weekend transport, dressed in their school uniform. It is not clear what happens to the Mama if her chick fails to gain university entrance.

【教育ママ】生存競争本能の権化。彼女たちの子供は、勉強漬けで窒息寸前である。ふつうの学校教育では満足できず、早朝に塾に、放課後に塾、そして夜も塾へと子供を追い立てる。かくして、深夜や週末の電車で立ったまま居眠りする、制服姿のあわれな子供たちができ上がる。子供が大学入試に落ちた時、ママはいったいどうなるのだろう。

The Permanent Office Fixture

There is one of these in every office. Most often an old school chum of the president, they appear to do little else than smoke and demand repeated refilling of their tea cups. This breed is spawned by the corporate seniority system which states, once a person reaches a suitable age, they are automatically promoted out of a job they can't do well into a job which they can't do at all.

【社内のお荷物】どの会社にも必ず1人はいる。社長の級友だったとかいう手合いが多く、タバコをふかして何杯もお茶をすする以外の仕事はあまりしていない。年功序列制度によって生き残り続けている。その制度によれば、ある年齢に達して困難になってきた職務から、全くできないので誰からも期待されない職務へと、昇進するようである。

The Umpire

A necessary evil which was spawned with the baseball cult/ritual. Some believe they are from the bat family due to their poor eyesight and also because they tend to get into a flap when confronted. Only have a limited vocabulary, punctuated by the two oaths, "Store-ra-ee-ku" and more often, "Aw-to"! Are very rarely interviewed on TV and never invited to summer or winter camps.

【アンパイヤ】野球試合をするための必要悪。視野に問題があり、カントクという敵に攻撃されると手をパタパタさせるので、祖先はコウモリ男だったとの説がある。語彙は乏しく、「ストラーイク！」か、もっと頻繁に発する「アーウト！」の呪いの言葉のみである。テレビでインタビューされることはまれで、球団の冬のキャンプに招かれることはさらにまれである。

The Masseur

Not to be confused with the female types operating in certain select areas of Japan, this male version can be found close by hot springs and bath houses. Equipped with tenacious talons, they are capable of detaching gristle from bone without tearing the flesh and appear to revel in the howls of agony from their clients. Don't plan to do anything for three days after a session.

【マッサージ師】しかるべき地域で活躍する、似た名前の職業の女性と混同しないように。こちらの方は、温泉やサウナ周辺がテリトリー。強靭な指で、肉をはがさずに軟骨を骨からはずす神ワザをこなし、客の悲痛なわめき声を無上の悦びとする。彼らにもんでもらったあと3日間は、自宅で安静にしているほうが利口というものだ。

The Centenarian

The real old crows of the species and their numbers are increasing annually. Per capita, there are more in Tokyo than in Osaka, and very few in the countryside. This has led to the firm belief that a high level of pollution contributes to living to a very old age, which is a bit of a serious setback for all the clean-air fanatics—as well as those strange folk who advocate non-smoking!

【百歳以上の高齢者】 この最高齢集団は、なんと年々増え続けている。大阪より東京に多く、片田舎には意外と少ない。ということは、公害がひどいほど老人の健康にはよいようである。公害排斥運動家や嫌煙家にとって、少々都合が悪いかもしれない事実だが……。

The Ordinary Policeman

Armed but rarely dangerous except if they ride into you on their bicycles. Appear to find foreigners transparent and breed in little hutches on most street corners. Very effective at creating chaotic traffic jams if traffic lights fail or if there is an accident. The female of the species can often be found in pairs in the tiniest of motor cars, hunting illegally parked vehicles.

【フツーの警官】武器は持っているものの、危険な存在ではない——自転車で通行人をひいたりしない限り。ガイジンは透明人間でもあるかのごとく無視する。拠点は交差点のちいさな小屋。信号の故障や交通事故があるたび、絶望的な渋滞をつくってあげるのが特技。この種の女性は、世界一小さな車に二人組で乗り、駐車違反を取り締まっている。

The Riot Policeman

Faceless, this species seems to breed at Narita Airport, however can often be found in cities whenever overseas VIP's are visiting. They are moved about in battleship grey busses with windows wired up to retain them. Never speak even if spoken to and by reputation, exceedingly violent.

【機動隊の警官】顔のないこの人種、成田付近に生息しているようだが、外国の要人が来日するたび都心にも現れる。移動する時は、窓に鉄の網を張った装甲車に乗り込む。話しかけられても決して口をきかず、ウワサによればきわめて暴力的でもあるという。

78

Miss "Whatever"

The most gorgeous of the female members of the species and quite often, remarkable curvy. Due to the male dominance of the species, there are numerous contests to find these females and their titles range from the sublime to the ridiculous, from resort names to the names of sanitary equipment manufacturers! Apparently their only required talent is to be able to look good in "hi-cut" swimwear.

【ミス・ナントカ】この国の女性の中では、最も見ためがよく、たいへん曲線的な体の持ち主たちである。いまだ男性優位なのか、この女性たちを生み出すコンテストはゴマンとある——ミス・○○○リゾートという高尚なものから、ミス・×××トイレ用品メーカーなんて馬鹿げたのまで。いうまでもなく、彼女たちに求められる唯一の才能は、ハイレグ水着が似合うこと。

The Fortune Teller

Preyed upon by the females of the species, these creatures sit in solitary splendor at small tables in disused shop and bank doorways, wearing dark glasses —even at night. They read palms, sticks and cards plus charge a fortune to read a fortune. The most famous one in Tokyo bears a sign stating, "Ingrish Spoking"!

【占い師】女性たちをいいカモにしているこの生物は、閉まった店や銀行の前にエラソーに陣取っている──夜でもサングラスをかけて。手相や棒きれやカードで彼らに占ってもらうウン勢は、料金もウンと高い。インチキな英語の看板を掲げているのには要注意。

The Gardener

A frightening breed, they look like characters from a second-rate horror movie. More tenacious than the Bonsai-ist they often only have minute little lairs in which to practice their pruning. Scrupulously tidy, they will pick up every tiny thing they clip and neatly tie it into bundles of precise size for disposal. Rarely operate spades because there is not enough earth.

【庭師】B級ホラー映画の登場人物のようで、コワイ人たち。ボンサイストより危険性のある彼らは、剪定の練習ももっぱら自宅で行う。切った枝は、ていねいに「普通ゴミ」サイズに束ねるところが裏ワザ。日本にはほとんど土がないため、すきはあまり使わない。

The Honeywagon Engineer

Detectable by day or night due to their distinctive odor, these are a breed which is rapidly disappearing from cities as technology about pumping the product uphill is advancing. Still to be seen/smelt in areas where homes are constructed among rice fields. If approached, will grunt, "Well somebody's gotter do it!" Not as financially secure as their counterparts in the Far East.

【くみとり車の作業員】独得な臭いですぐわかるこの人種は、テクノロジーの発達とともに都会から姿を消しつつある。とはいえ、家が田んぼに囲まれている地域では、いまだ健在――「結局、誰かがやらなきゃいけないんだ……」とブツブツ言いながらも。極東の他の国々の同業者に比べ、今後の生活は保障されていない。

The Golf-aholic

Will willingly join a queue at 2 a.m., to play one round on a public golf course, which costs only ¥15,000 (Only!). Spends every weekend, lovingly cleaning his clubs and putting a shine on his balls. Can recite every stroke at every game he has played and if unable to get a game, will merrily hit balls into the air at a practice range, day or night.

【ゴルフ狂】公営ゴルフ場で1ラウンドたった1万5千円(たったのだって!?)でプレーするためならば、午前2時からの行列もいとわない。週末には必ず、さもいとおしそうにクラブを磨く。これまでにプレーしたどのゲームのどのショットをも、克明に覚えている人々。コースを予約できなかった日でも、喜々として打ちっぱなしを楽しんでいる。

The Rabbit Hutch

These dwellings are often called "bird cages" due to the walls giving just about the same level of privacy to the occupants. This tiny area in which to live has created the myth about this being the reason why the species are rather short in stature, can sit with their legs folded up, roll up their beds in the day and cultivate bonsai. It's a matter of which came first!

【ウサギ小屋】居住者のプライバシーなどないに等しいことから、鳥カゴとも呼ばれている。この国の人々が、背が低く、正座ができ、毎朝フトンをたたみ、盆栽を生み出したのは、この小さな住空間のせいであるという者も多い。しかしこんなの、ニワトリか卵かと同じ問題じゃないか!

The Matchmaker

This particular group has been around for centuries, proffering assistance to the parents of unwed offspring. Once they were the only method used to match pairs, however nowadays, various other means are used as well. Computerization has appeared allowing huge data banks to be created of those wishing to meet each other; also, many of the species now actually fall in love.

【仲人オバサン】何世紀にもわたり、未婚の子供を持つ親の強力な味方となってきた。昔は男女の縁をとりもつ唯一の存在として活躍したが、現在では他にも手段があるので、影が薄くなりつつある。コンピューター結婚相談所は豊富なデータで成果をあげているし、なんとホントに恋愛する人も多くなったとか。

Sentō

The public bird bath of the species. Once for mixed sexes, those types are rare nowadays. Irrespective of the heat of the water, the species will gather daily in a ritualistic manner to launder the local gossip and to relax after a hard day avoiding the boss, wife, etc. Regulars always carry their own shampoo.

【銭湯】まるで鳥のようだが、日本には公衆浴場が存在する。現代ではまれになったが、昔は混浴が多かったそうで、うらやましい限り。近所のウワサ話を楽しみ、上司や奥方をしばし忘れてくつろぐために、煮え湯のような熱さをものともせず、人々はここに集うのである。

The Schoolboy Commuter

Carries a bulging shoulder bag and travels in small groups. Since the advent of fast foods, this species has become startlingly tall. They retain the plumage of ancient Japanese militia, however their footwear usually has the heel kicked down and is worn like a slipper.

【男子中・高生】ふくらんだカバンを肩に掛け、小さな集団で通学する。ファーストフードの到来以降、彼らの身長はみるみる伸びた。制服は古臭い軍服のようだが、クツの方はかかとを踏みつぶしてスリッパのようなのが興味深い。

The Bald Ego

Because most natives are relatively the same height, this species is most often noticed by foreigners who are slightly taller. Strands of hair are laid across the bald pate to create the illusion of thatch. Their appearance from above is identical to the Universal Product Code label number, 6-123456789 0-2. They can hear rain before most others notice it is raining.

【ハゲ頭の抵抗】他の日本人は彼と同じくらいの背丈なのでよく見えないが、やや背の高いガイジンはこの人種を見やぶってしまう。「ススキ頭」という幻視トリックを使っているが、上から見下ろせば、これはバーコード以外の何物でもない。まわりの人たちより、いち早く雨が降り始めたことがわかる。頭皮に降る雨は、意外とウルサイのである。

88

The Oba-san

Can enter and exit any level of crowded conveyance. Deft with umbrellas, shopping bags or just plain elbows, if you are stuck in a rush hour train just follow the swathe they carve through the mob. They are equipped with a sharp tongue and can castigate any species with equal venom. Add a new dimension to the term, "Sweet little old ladies"!

【オバサン】どんなに混んだバスや電車でも、難なく乗り降りできる人々のこと。もしあなたが満員電車で身動きがとれなくなったら、オバサンについて行けばよい。カサや買物袋やひじテツで簡単に通り道を作っていくのだから。また、彼女たちの毒舌はすさまじいので注意されたし。いずれにせよ、「オバサン恐るべし」!

The Olympian

Startlingly young, these chicks are imbued with the competitive spirit from birth. "Go for the Gold" rings in their ears almost before they are able to talk. Can be seen at every park and public swimming pool, usually pursued by at least one parent, shouting encouragement. Most grow into salarymen or OL's and a few into athletes.

【オリンピックをめざす少年少女】 まだ幼いヒヨコたちだが、生まれた時から競争精神をたたきこまれている。「金を勝ち取れ」という言葉が、まだ話せないうちから耳の中で鳴り響いている。公園や公営プールで、熱心すぎる親に激励されながら練習に明け暮れる日々。だがそのほとんどは長じて平凡な会社員となり、選手になるものはごく少数である。

The Child Actress

All appear to have mis-cast teeth and smile continuously. This species is amazingly calm and self-controlled when doing anything from simply walking around to "singing" into a microphone bigger than they can grasp in one hand. Surprisingly, quite a number of them have a remarkable level of talent.

【ちびっ子タレント】例外なく歯並びが悪いのに、始終ニッコリと笑顔をつくる少女たちのこと。驚くほど冷静で自己をコントロールできるため、何でもやってのける。単に歩いてみせたり、自分の手でつかめないくらい大きなマイクで「歌」と称するものを披露したり……。驚くべきことに、彼女たちの多くは、実はかなりのレベルの才能をもっている。

Beer Jokki

A container available in many different sizes which all appear to hold the same amount of liquid. They are considered full when the froth reaches the rim and the beer, the top of the handle. As beer is one of the major lubricants of the species, the four brewers constantly compete by introducing new brands—often 5 each every year. Surely, "dry beer" is a contradiction of words?!

【ビア・ジョッキ】この容器にはいろいろなサイズとデザインが出回っているが、どれも入る量に差などなさそうである。泡の表面がふちまで来ていて、把手の上まで液体が入ってさえいれば、満杯だとされてしまう。ビールが人間関係の潤滑油となっているこの国では、毎年、4大メーカーがそれぞれ少なくとも5種類は新製品を発売する。それにしても「禁酒の」ビールとは、きついシャレのつもりか!?

The Fish Buyer

Before dawn's early light, take a trip to Tsukiji fish market and join the hundreds of bidders. Don't raise your hand or you might become the proud owner of a fish, longer than you are tall. Embarrassing on the subway and as difficult as heck to stuff into your refrigerator.

【魚の競売】夜明け前に築地魚市場へ行って何百人の競り手に混じってみよう。しかし調子に乗りすぎてうっかり手を上げたりすると、自分の身長より長い魚を買い取るハメになる。どうにか地下鉄に乗れたとしても、自宅の冷蔵庫に収まるわけがないではないか。

The English Student

Tend to follow foreigners and rarely seen without a textbook in hand. Will speak without being spoken to and sound remarkably like pre-recorded tapes. Most have American accents, but these days, a few with Australian, French, German and even English accents can be heard.

【英会話学校の生徒】片時もテキストを離さず、ガイジンにまとわりついては話しかけてくる。それも、会話レッスン用テープそっくりの話し方で。大半はアメリカ英語だが、昨今はオーストラリアやフランス、ドイツのなまりがあったり、驚くべきことにクイーンズ・イングリッシュを話す者までいる。

Late Night Library

Found by nearly every railway station, this is a chance for the lone wolf to pick his night time reading without others seeing what he chooses. None of the publications are in English; mind you most of them don't need any descriptive text at all. These "magazines" are never carried in public without them being in plain, brown paper covers.

【夜の図書館】駅周辺には必ずある。独身男性にとって、自分の選んだ本を他人に知られることなく、夜の読書タイムを充実させてくれる強い味方だ。英語版は一冊もないが、どうせ文章なんて読む必要はないので、きちんと役に立つ。こういう「雑誌」は地味な紙で包まない限り、人前で持ち歩かないように。

The Rice Ball

Never in the shape of a ball, unless made by children, these are almost the staple diet of the nation. Wrapped in a sheet of dried kelp, the contents vary from items most foreigners would consider edible (cooked tuna) to some things, even a hardened traveller would prefer not to put in their mouth (*nattō*).

【おにぎり】「ライス・ボール」といったって、子供がにぎったのでもない限り、球形はしていない。日本人の主食の一つであり、のりで包んだのが一般的。中身のほうは多様で、ガイジンにも食べられるもの（ツナ）もあれば、いろいろな国の食べ物を経験してきたツワモノでも敬遠するもの（納豆）もある。

The College Student

This breed appears to smoke, play pachinko and mahjong and never ever study. Can be found in crowds, milling about in front of universities, nearby railway stations, ice cream parlors and fast food outlets. Most appear to have money, but surprisingly few drink alcohol in public.

【大学生】この人種はみな、タバコを吸いパチンコと麻雀をやり、そして何より絶対に勉強などしない。大学周辺や駅、アイスクリーム屋とかファーストフード店にたむろしている。お金はあるようだが、外ではあまり酒を飲まないようだ。

Exam Hell Ritual

The annual Right of Passage ritual which is pressure-induced torture to gain a position at any university. Held every February, it appears to be a Government sponsored tradition to keep cram schools in business and feather the nests of unemployed teachers who work at night.

【大学入試】 大学に入るために必ず受けなければならない、拷問のようなもの。予備校を繁盛させ夜間働く講師たちを養うために毎年2月に政府が主催するイベントである。

High School Baseball Tourney Ritual

Twice every year, every high school is forced to play against each other for the pleasure of the television cameras and millions of viewers. Doesn't appear to serve any useful purpose, other than being a vehicle for advertising and giving out of work baseball commentators, something to do.

【高校野球】テレビカメラと全国の視聴者を喜ばせるために行う、年2回の催し。広告スペースを提供し、ひまな野球解説者に仕事を与える以外には、有益な目的はないようだ。

98

The TV Caster

Always exceedingly excited about everything from an 80 kilometer traffic jam to the latest antics of Ueno Zoo's pandas. Can spend 10 minutes talking about a traffic accident while pointing at chalk marks on the street. Never ever seem to get out of breath and keep their voices pitched an octave above the rest of the species.

【ニュースキャスター】80キロの交通渋滞から上野動物園のパンダまで、何についても異常にコーフンして語る人々。現場に残るチョークの線を指さして、事故について10分間もしゃべり続けられるのはお見事。決して息が切れたりせず、ふつうの人より1オクターブ声も高い。

Golf Widow

Truly, the happiest of the female of the species. Her rooster disappears each Saturday and Sunday from before dawn to after dusk and usually returns to the nest tired but sober. She has the place to herself all weekend to do whatever she wants to—which is usually the laundry, or futon beating, or cleaning or cooking.

【ゴルフ・ウィドウ】皮肉なんかじゃなく、日本で一番幸せな女たち。夫は毎週末になると、早朝からゴルフに出かけて夜遅くまで帰ってこない。おかげで彼女たちは、ジャマをされずにやりたいことができるわけだ――洗たくとかフトン干しとか、そうじに料理などを。

The Comic Book

The addiction of the whole species, these picture books with words are about everything imaginable from pure science fiction to starting your own company and many are startlingly violent and/or pornographic. Children's versions abound and it is very irritating for foreigners to observe tiny kids who can actually read them!

【マンガ本】日本人はみなマンガ中毒である。このセリフ入り絵本の内容は多彩で、ＳＦや「会社のおこし方」などというのもあるが、多くは暴力とセックス過剰。子供向けのマンガとなると、星の数ほどもある。まだ小さな子供がマンガ本を面白そうに読む姿は、読めないガイジンにとって実にクヤシイのだ。

The Shopper

Due to the incredible lack of storage space in the average nest, the species is a daily shopper. Goods are sold either singly or in Lilliputian sizes and often more than triple wrapped. A departure from the norm are toilet rolls which seem to come in packs of at least 16! It is unknown what other uses the species has for them.

【買い物客】 収納スペースが十分にないので、日本人は毎日買い物をする。外国と違って、商品はバラ売りや小パックで売られ、また三重以上の過剰包装が常識。ただ一つ極小サイズでないのは、16ロールもあるトイレットペーパー！ 本来の使用目的以外、いったい何に使うというのだ。

The Bank Lobby Lady

Always welcoming and bidding adieu to customers, this species is quick to appear beside any native having problems but usually vanishes if a foreigner gets into difficulty. Once captured, they can never speak English but shake their heads and suck their teeth a lot. Never seem to have machine instructions in English.

103

【銀行のロビー係】 ひっきりなしに客にあいさつをするこの人種は、日本人が何か困っている様子だとすっ飛んでくるが、ガイジンが同じ状況にいる時は姿を消している。たとえつかまえたとしても、英語は全く話さず、しきりに首を振ったり歯の間からシーシーと音をたてるのみ。自動振込み機の操作を英語で説明できる者は皆無のようだ。

Vertical Society

The pecking order in Japan is well defined: Progress in anything is straight up and down. When you are old enough, you automatically climb the corporate ladder. At school or at play, you never associate with those beyond your station in life, above or below. Even the language style used changes with the status of the talker and the talkee. Lateral thinkers appear to have flown the coup.

【タテ型社会】日本は明確な序列社会だ。企業においては、ある年齢になると昇進の階段が用意されている。子供だって、学校や遊びの場で年と違う子たちと接することは少ない。言葉づかいすら、相手との上下関係によって変える。しかるに水平思考のできる者は、この社会を見限って脱出してしまう。

The Noodle Slurper

Can be seen at any time of the day or night, noisily inhaling white hot noodles, either at streetside stalls or in shoebox-sized shops. In the evening, these are quite often nocturnal pub-crawlers trying not to become obnoxious drunks—with varying success. Should be observed from a distance unless you are planning to throw away your clothes.

【ソバをズルズルすする人】屋台やくつ箱ほどの大きさの店で、アツアツのソバをすすり上げる人たちの姿は、昼夜問わず見かけられる。夜は酔っぱらいが酔いざましによく使う手段である——効果のほどはさまざまだが。自分の服をおシャカにする覚悟がない限り、あまり近寄って観察するのは避けた方がよろしい。

The Economist

This breed always answers questions with questions. Can quote exchange rates to three decimal places in five different currencies. They are never certain of the future and often mumble terms like, "Oil Shock" or "Bubble Economy" when talking about the money market. It is uncertain if they ever invest any of their own money.

【経済学者】この人種はいつも、質問に質問で答える。5種類の通貨の為替レートを、コンマ3ケタまで正確に言えるのが自慢。将来についての確信は何もなく、市場を語るときは「オイル・ショック」だの「バブル経済」だのと便利な言葉を多用する。彼らが自分のおカネを少しでも投資しているのかどうかは、さだかではない。

The Wedding Photo

A stereotype pose, handed down from generation to generation, designed to show that the newlyweds are already aware they will never be able to own their own home unless they can have children who also have children, so that they can get a father, son and grandson mortgage. Spend the first two years of married life paying off the wedding ceremony debt.

【結婚写真】子孫に残される、決まりきったポーズの写真。自分の子供がまた子供をつくって三世代ローンを組める確信がない限り、マイホームはぜったい無理だということを、写真の新婚夫婦の表情はもの語っている。最初の2年間は、挙式費用の返済に明け暮れる結婚生活でもある。

The Overseas Vacationer

The most well recognized member of the species which can be found in duty-free stores as far apart as Anchorage and Sydney, or Los Angles and Schipol. Mostly migrate all together at New Year, Golden Week (May) and the summer *Obon* holiday (August) periods. Spend a lot of money, mostly on presents for those who don't go overseas.

【海外旅行者】アンカレッジやシドニー、ＬＡ、スキポルなど、世界中の免税店でお目にかかれる日本人のこと。年末年始とゴールデンウィーク、それとお盆休みに大挙して外国へ行く。海外に行かなかった友人のお土産に、大金を使って帰ってくる。

The Bicycle

Fitted with advanced-warning brake pads whose squeak can dislodge every tooth filling in your head, these machines congregate around stations, are cleared away by the police from time to time and reappear immediately. Ridden along the footpath, they have priority over pedestrians and are exceedingly dangerous.

【自転車】警告ブレーキなる秘密兵器でキーキーといやな音をたてるこの機械は、駅前にたくさん放置されている。警察が時たま排除するものの、数日後にはまた、同じ状態に戻ってしまう。歩道を走る自転車は、通行人の安全を大いに脅かしている。

The Athlete

Constructed of skin, bone and muscles, this breed always looks like some refugee from a famine plagued land. In Japan there are marathons almost every week, so these athletes never get much time to regain the weight they lose by jogging behind police motorbikes, inhaling photochemical fog.

110

【陸上選手】この人種の体は骨と皮と筋肉だけでできているので、まるで大飢饉のあった国から来た難民のように見える。日本では毎週のようにマラソン大会が行われるが、気の毒なことだ。先導する白バイの排気ガスを大量に吸って体重を減らしてしまう選手たちは、回復する余裕もないにちがいない。

The Heavy Smoker

A natural habit of the species, some can reach four packs a day, but often only take a couple of puffs and then put the cigarette out. Now, this breed has been officially relegated to "Smoking Zones" on the JR Yamanote Line when authorities found out that simply removing the ashtrays didn't stop them. They merely threw the butts on the tracks.

111

【ヘビー・スモーカー】この国では、喫煙はごく自然な行為。一日4箱に及ぶ者もいるが、そのほとんどは少しふかしてはもみ消しているようだ。近頃、JR山手線のホームでは「喫煙所」へと追いやられている。何故なら、ただ灰皿をなくしただけでは、彼らは少しもひるまなかったからである——吸いがらは線路に投げ捨てていたのだ。

The Fashion Statement

A backlash against the traditional kimono has caused a wave of this expressive clothing to appear. Termed the "Youth Culture Fashion" it has about as much resemblance to "Haute Couture" as *enka* songs have to rock and roll. Some astonishing use of English can be discovered by the serious observer.

【ファッション】長かったキモノ文化の反動で、自己表現する洋服が台頭した。とはいえ「渋カジ」と「オート・クチュール」は演歌とロックほどの差があるのも否めない。ときどき、ブランド名やロゴに呆れるほどまちがった英語を使っている。

Simultaneous Translator

Sound operated voice machines, this breed can think ahead into the thought pattern of those they are listening to and talk at the same time as they are listening. Because a Japanese sentence can turn into a question with the very last syllable, the speakers sometimes end a statement with the words, "Isn't it?"

【同時通訳者】音声を出す機械のような人々。話す者の思考パターンを先読みして、聞くと同時に話すことができる。日本語は最後の一字でイキナリ質問文に変貌するため、英語に通訳しているほうは、あわてて "Isn't it?" (ですね?)と付け加えることになるのだ。

Motorcycle Terrorist

A breed that appears almost impossible to stamp out, these *bōsōzoku* bozos drive around quiet streets at night, engines at full rev, with no mufflers. Sometimes alone but often in a group, they never appear to operate on the normal streets where the traffic jams would allow the policeman on his push-bike to catch them!

【バイクに乗ったテロリスト】暴走族と呼ばれ、外見も手ごわそうである。マフラーを取り、エンジン全開で夜の静寂をぶちこわしてくれる。集団行動が大好きな彼らだが、日中はあまり活動しない。というのも渋滞がひどくて、自転車に乗ったおまわりさんにパクられてしまうからである。

Bōnenkai

Traditional, year-end gift giving and party time. After the third party the same evening, some can be seen in small groups who can defy gravity although their bodies appear to lack any bones. Often change into some form of karaoke warbler for a period before finally emerging as Greater or Lesser Obnoxious Drunks for the trip home.

【忘年会】毎年、師走になると催される酒盛り。三次会を過ぎた頃には、体がぐにゃぐにゃになりながらも、必死に重力に抵抗している人々が見かけられる。途中でカラオケ大会と化し、最終的には皆へべれけになって家路につくのがお決まりのコース。

Samurai Actor

Never smile and really look quite frightening. Appear to be able to see through the back of their heads when engaged in swordfights. Their voices are pitched two octaves below the other actors, and they are usually taller and incredibly fit. If killed, take a very long time to die. Never kiss.

【時代劇俳優】 いつもオソロシイ形相をしていて、笑顔をふりまいたりはしない。チャンバラ・シーンでは、自分の背後を透視する能力を発揮する。わき役に比べて2オクターブも声が低く、反対に背は高くてスマート。殺される時は、長い長い時間をかけて息をひきとる。キス・シーンは演じない。

The Rugby Player

Look very tiny when alongside Wallabies or All Blacks, this species is cheered wildly at the Hong Kong Sevens—but usually lose. Younger ones can be found at any weekend, practicing their art on riverbanks—even in mid winter with snow on the ground.

【ラグビー選手】ワラビーズやオール・ブラックスに交じると、子供のように小さく見える。それでもホンコン・セブンスでは熱狂的な応援を受けている——たいてい負けてしまうが。週末、若い選手たちが河川敷で練習に打ち込んでいるのをよく見る。真冬には、泥まじりの雪にまみれてまで。

Omiai (The Arranged Marriage)

A classic native custom which allows for elderly members of the species to decide the pairing arrangements in a way where the offspring get no say in the matter. Some observers believe this custom is designed to allow the couple to lead completely separate lives under the same roof but sometimes it works!

【お見合い】子供の意見に耳をかさずに、親たちが勝手に縁組を結ぶこともできる、伝統ある習慣。ひとつ屋根の下で、男女が他人のように別々な生活を送るように仕組むものだと言う人もいる。しかし、そんな結婚生活も意外と成立するのだ！

Gas Station Girl

Always cheerful, will clean windows without being asked. These members of the species appear to be all related to one another because they all look the same. They will welcome you upon arrival and not only gush thanks on your departure but will hold up traffic to allow you to get your car back into the traffic jam.

【ガソリンスタンドの女子店員】必要以上に陽気で、頼まれてもいないのに車の窓を磨く。彼女たちは全員、姉妹やイトコ同士だと思われる——みな同じ顔をしているのだ。客の車が入ると出迎え、出ていく時は「ありがとう」を連呼するのはわかる。しかし、身を挺してまで車を渋滞道路に割り込ませる手伝いをするのはスゴイ。

Yakitori Chef

This breed can be found all over the place, usually in shoe box sized stores, hunched over a brazier while they barbecue indescribable bits of chicken or pig. Their nests are often coated in a layer of grease although the serving areas are squeaky clean. Can be found by sniffing the air for burning chicken fat.

【ヤキトリ屋のオヤジ】くつ箱ほどの大きさの店を構えて、炭火の煙にいぶされながら、トリのとても口では言えないような部位の肉を焼いている。店の壁や柱は油でギトギトなのに、客席はきれいになっているのが不思議。トリの脂肪のこげるにおいで、すぐに居所がかぎわけられる人々。

The Story Teller

This breed is capable of sitting on its heels for hours and talking continuously. They are considered screamingly funny by other members of the species and often take part in contests. To many foreigners who understand the language, their tales are not the least bit funny. Japanese nuance doesn't translate.

【落語家】この人種は、長時間正座をしながらしゃべりまくることができる。日本人は彼らの話に腹をかかえて笑う。落語家のコンテストもある。しかし、日本語のわかるガイジンでも、彼らの面白さはなかなかわからない。日本語のシャレやオチは伝わりにくいようだ。

The White Surgical Masked Man

As winter closes in, this breed begins to appear. By mid winter there are at least half a dozen on every form of public transport. They don't talk much and appear to cough and sneeze a lot. Nearly all of them would not know which end of a scalpel to pick up, let alone how to tie a knot in a suture.

【白マスクの男】冬がやってくると、この連中が台頭する。真冬には電車やバスに乗り合わせた人のうち5〜6人は必ずコレである。あまりしゃべらず、やたら咳やくしゃみをする。外科用メスの持ち方や傷口の縫い合わせ方を知っている者は皆無に等しいのに、なぜ医療用マスクをしているのか不可解。

Baseball Nest

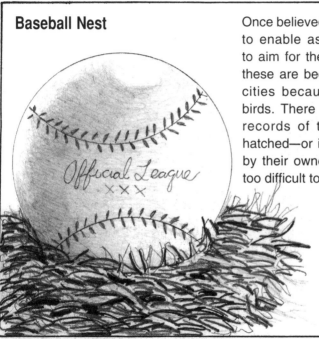

Official League
× × ×

Once believed to be a form of shrine to enable aspiring baseball stars to aim for the "homer" of the year, these are becoming a rare sight in cities because there are so few birds. There have been no written records of the balls ever being hatched—or in fact, being retrieved by their owners. Trees are usually too difficult to climb.

【野球ボールの巣】 未来の野球選手たちがホームラン王になるための神殿と言われていたが、都会に鳥がほとんどいない今では、鳥の巣にボールが収まっている光景も珍しくなりつつある。ボールがここで孵化したという記録はないし、実際持ち主が取り戻しに行ったということもない—大抵の木は枝が切られていて登れないのだ。

The Chikan

Usually migrate into flocks of hens and chicks where there are ample tail feathers to caress. It is believed that there are more of these than meet the eye due to the fact that females of the species rarely complain aloud about this form of harassment. The occasional Chikan who plies his trade overseas will either get a stiletto heel through his foot or at very least a black eye.

【チカン】 触わりたくなるような柔らかい羽毛のメンドリやヒヨコたちの群れに、好んで入っていく人種。この国の女性は、このようなイカガワシイ行為に対して大声で抵抗することが少ないので、バイ菌のごとくはびこっている。外国でこんなことをしようものなら、針のようなハイヒールで思いっきり足を踏まれるか、目のまわりに青アザをつくるのがオチである。

Crows and Pigeons

The only winged population of all cities. Due to the comparatively low level of rubbish in the streets, some observers believe these birds can eat concrete, bitumen and cigarette butts. It is certain however that they can breath photochemical fog. They are usually silent and awesome until you want to sleep in on a Sunday morning when they will invariably become raucous and a pain in the ear.

【カラスとハト】都会に住む唯一の鳥類。道ばたにあまりゴミがない日本では、この鳥たちはコンクリートやアスファルト、それにタバコの吸いがらを主食にしていると言われる。とにかく、排気ガスを吸って生きているのは事実。ふだんは恐れ多いほど静かだが、人々が日曜日の朝寝坊を決めこんだとたん、きまってギャーギャーと耳をつんざく不敵な鳥でもある。

The Card Exchange Ritual

In a land where male plumage doesn't vary, this ritual is performed upon first meeting any other male as a means of discovering status. Then, the angle of bow and the type of language to be used are preset according to ancient protocol. The cards received are fanned out in front of one so one can remember just whom the other people are.

【名刺交換の儀式】男性の服装に自己表現のないこの国では、初対面の男同士が相手のステイタスを知るために欠かせないもの。この儀式を行ってから、お辞儀の角度や言葉づかいを決める。座ってからも、相手の名前を忘れないよう、テーブルに名刺を置いたまま話を続ける。

The Scholar

Very talkative and often quite boring, this species appears on a rostrum at every wedding or public function. National TV always invites them to speak about everything from why the NIKKEI index rises/falls to what is right/wrong about the British Royal family.

【学者】スピーチができると聞けば、結婚式だろうが公共機関だろうが、どこにでも現れる、非常におしゃべりで退屈な人種。国営（？）放送は彼らを頻繁に出演させ、日経インデックスの上昇・下降から、英国王室の賛否にいたるもろもろの閑話をさせている。

The Happy Commuter

This breed is probably born on the trains because they always have a seat, which automatically gives them enough space to open a newspaper. Appear to be seething internally at what they read, but it is usually only a sign that their favorite baseball team is on a losing streak. Always in a suit.

【幸福な通勤族】新聞を広げるスペースのある座席に、いつも陣取っている。ということは、電車の中で生まれた人々らしい。読んでいる記事に憤慨しているように見えるのは、応援する野球チームが連敗しているからにすぎない場合が多い。つねに背広姿。

The Lesser Panda

Delightful, cute and cuddly, but beyond these attributes, bear little resemblance to the giant panda. This species learns how to speak and can often be seen playing in the company of different species without being at all shy. When older, sometimes join Disneyland but most become salarymen or OL's. It is believed, some become politicians.

【レッサー・パンダ】明るくかわいく無邪気だが、それ以外はジャイアントパンダにはほとんど似ていない。この動物には、誰とでも臆面なく話し、ところかまわず図々しく遊ぶ術がある。そんな資質を生かして、大人になるとディズニーランドで働いたり政治家になる者もいるようだが、たいていはサラリーマンやOLになる。

The White Tailed Tennis Player

A caged member of the species seen at most municipal centers from dawn to dusk. Often use both hands to swing their rackets and have at least 100 balls scattered around their cage. Always look extremely serious when actually hitting an airborne ball and rarely talk to each other.

【白いシッポのテニスプレーヤー】 オリの中を好み、どんな公営コートにもたくさんいる。両手打ちが得意な点、それにオリのまわりに100個ほどのボールを散乱させる点なども特徴。飛んできた球を打つ時の表情は深刻そのもので、不気味なほど黙々とプレーする人々。

The "WAA" Children

Nicknamed "Half" children by the natives because these are the offspring of one Japanese and one foreign parent, these inhabitants are a species on their own. Usually totally bicultural and bilingual, they can eat any type of food, see situations from two different sides, have twice the capacity to find things amusing and are often more than two times as bright as many of their contemporaries. They should be renamed "Double" children.

【「ハーフ」の子供たち】日本人とガイジンの親から生まれたので、この国ではそう呼ばれている子供たち。しかし実は、彼らは独自の人種なのだ。その多くが二つの言語と二つの文化を完全に理解し、どんな国の食べ物も食べられ、物事を二面的に見て、人生を楽しむ術を持つ。他の人間より数倍アタマもよかったりする。というわけで、「ハーフ」ではなく「ダブル」と呼ぶにふさわしい存在なのである。

The Observers

Foreigners (married to native lasses) who are often simply tolerated rather than accepted into the species. Will amaze some folk when they use chopsticks lefthanded or eat ethnic food and dumbfound all by occasionally mumbling oaths in Japanese. Used to try to change the system but now, just smile a lot.

【日本人ウォッチャー】 ガイジン（日本人と結婚している場合が多い）。日本人は喜んで彼らを受け入れているというより、黙認しているようである。左利きでハシを使えば面白がられ、タクワンや納豆を食べれば意外な顔をされ、ちょっとでも日本語を話せば腰を抜かして驚かれる。若い頃は日本人や日本社会を自分が変えようとやっきになったが、今ではただニンマリと笑って事態をながめるばかりだ。

THE JAPANESE : A FIELD GUIDE

1992年11月5日 初版発行

著　者　ティム・エルンスト／マイク・マークルー
　　　　©1992 by T. Ernst & M. Marklew
発行者　太田　良久
発行所　株式会社　ジャパン　タイムズ
　　　　〒108　東京都港区芝浦4丁目5番4号
　　　　電話　東京(03) 3453-2013 ［出版営業］
　　　　　　　　　　 3453-2797 ［出版編集］

　　　　振替口座　東京9-64848
印刷所　株式会社　太平印刷社

カバーデザイン：(株)CADEC
定価はカバーに表示してあります。

ISBN4-7890-0660-3